West Virginia Ecoregions

- ☐ Western Allegheny Plateau
- ■ Central Appalachians
- ▨ Ridge and Valley

Charleston

1. Altona Marsh
2. Sleepy Creek Wildlife Management Area
3. Canaan Valley State Park
4. Dolly Sods & Bear Rock
5. Spruce Knob Area
6. Gaudineer Knob Scenic Area
7. Cranberry Glades
8. Stonewall Jackson Lake
9. Greenbrier River Trail
10. Babcock State Park
11. Bluestone State Park
12. Brush Creek Watershed
13. R.D. Bailey Lake
14. Twin Falls State Park
15. Coonskin Park
16. Beech Fork Lake & State Park
17. Greenbottom Wildlife Management Area
18. Ohio River Islands National Wildlife Refuge
19. North Bend State Park
20. Oglebay Park
21. Core Arboretum
22. Cranesville Swamp
23. Pleasant Creek Wildlife Management Area
24. Audra State Park

A POCKET NATURALIST® GUIDE

WEST VIRGINIA BIRDS – A Folding Pocket Guide to Familiar Species

WATERFORD PRESS

WEST VIRGINIA BIRDS

A Folding Pocket Guide to Familiar Species

Pied-billed Grebe
Podilymbus podiceps
To 13 in. (33 cm)

Common Loon
Gavia immer To 3 ft. (90 cm)
Winter / Summer

Horned Grebe
Podiceps auritus
To 15 in. (38 cm)

Canada Goose
Branta canadensis
To 45 in. (1.14 m)

Tundra Swan
Cygnus columbianus
To 4.5 ft. (1.4 m)
Note yellow mark on black bill.

American Black Duck
Anas rubripes
To 25 in. (63 cm)

Northern Pintail
Anas acuta To 30 in. (75 cm)

Wood Duck
Aix sponsa
To 20 in. (50 cm)

Northern Shoveler
Spatula clypeata To 20 in. (50 cm)
Named for its large spatulate bill.

Mallard
Anas platyrhynchos
To 28 in. (70 cm)

Green-winged Teal
Anas crecca To 15 in. (38 cm)

Blue-winged Teal
Spatula discors To 16 in. (40 cm)
Male's white facial crescent is distinctive.

American Wigeon
Mareca americana To 23 in. (58 cm)

Redhead
Aythya americana
To 22 in. (55 cm)

Ring-necked Duck
Aythya collaris To 18 in. (45 cm)
Note white ring near bill tip.

White-winged Scoter
Melanitta fusca To 23 in. (58 cm)
Note white wing patches.

Canvasback
Aythya valisineria To 2 ft. (60 cm)
Note sloping forehead and black bill.

Common Goldeneye
Bucephala clangula To 18 in. (45 cm)
Male has a white facial spot.

Bufflehead
Bucephala albeola
To 15 in. (38 cm)

Ruddy Duck
Oxyura jamaicensis
To 16 in. (40 cm)

Hooded Merganser
Lophodytes cucullatus
To 20 in. (50 cm)

Red-breasted Merganser
Mergus serrator To 27 in. (68 cm)

American Coot
Fulica americana
To 16 in. (40 cm)

Lesser Scaup
Aythya affinis To 18 in. (45 cm)

Killdeer
Charadrius vociferus
To 12 in. (30 cm)
Note two breast bands.

Greater Yellowlegs
Tringa melanoleuca
To 15 in. (38 cm)

Woodcock
Scolopax rusticola
To 15 in. (38 cm)

Green Heron
Butorides virescens
To 22 in. (55 cm)

Wilson's Snipe
Gallinago delicata
To 12 in. (30 cm)

Black-crowned Night-Heron
Nycticorax nycticorax
To 28 in. (70 cm)

Great Blue Heron
Ardea herodias
To 4.5 ft. (1.4 m)

Double-crested Cormorant
Phalacrocorax auritus
To 3 ft. (90 cm)

Great Egret
Ardea alba
To 38 in. (95 cm)

Bonaparte's Gull
Chroicocephalus philadelphia
To 14 in. (35 cm)
Small, black-headed gull.

Ring-billed Gull
Larus delawarensis
To 20 in. (50 cm)
Bill has dark ring.

Herring Gull
Larus argentatus
To 26 in. (65 cm)
Black wing tips are white-spotted. Legs are pinkish.

DOVES, WOODPECKERS, ETC.

Mourning Dove
Zenaida macroura
To 13 in. (33 cm)

Rock Pigeon
Columba livia
To 13 in. (33 cm)
Common in urban areas.

Yellow-billed Cuckoo
Coccyzus americanus
To 14 in. (35 cm)

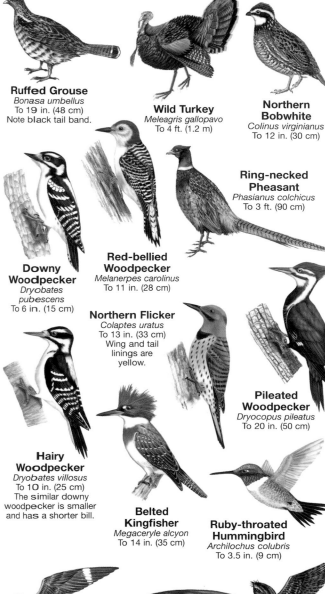

DOVES, WOODPECKERS, ETC.

Ruffed Grouse
Bonasa umbellus
To 19 in. (48 cm)
Note black tail band.

Wild Turkey
Meleagris gallopavo
To 4 ft. (1.2 m)

Northern Bobwhite
Colinus virginianus
To 12 in. (30 cm)

Downy Woodpecker
Dryobates pubescens
To 6 in. (15 cm)

Red-bellied Woodpecker
Melanerpes carolinus
To 11 in. (28 cm)

Ring-necked Pheasant
Phasianus colchicus
To 3 ft. (90 cm)

Northern Flicker
Colaptes auratus
To 13 in. (33 cm)
Wing and tail linings are yellow.

Hairy Woodpecker
Dryobates villosus
To 10 in. (25 cm)
The similar downy woodpecker is smaller and has a shorter bill.

Pileated Woodpecker
Dryocopus pileatus
To 20 in. (50 cm)

Belted Kingfisher
Megaceryle alcyon
To 14 in. (35 cm)

Ruby-throated Hummingbird
Archilochus colubris
To 3.5 in. (9 cm)

Common Nighthawk
Chordeiles minor
To 10 in. (25 cm)
Often hawks for insects around street lights.

Chimney Swift
Chaetura pelagica
To 6 in. (15 cm)
Appears to beat wings alternately in flight.

Whip-poor-will
Antrostomus vociferus
To 10 in. (25 cm)
Its rhythmic call – whip-poor-will – can be heard at night.

Turkey Vulture
Cathartes aura
To 32 in. (80 cm)

Red-tailed Hawk
Buteo jamaicensis
To 25 in. (63 cm)

Cooper's Hawk
Accipiter cooperii
To 20 in. (50 cm)
Note long, rounded tail.

Broad-winged Hawk
Buteo platypterus
To 19 in. (48 cm)
Note dark and light tail bands.

Sharp-shinned Hawk
Accipiter striatus
To 14 in. (35 cm)
Note long, square-edged tail and striped breast.

Red-shouldered Hawk
Buteo lineatus
To 22 in. (55 cm)

Northern Harrier
Circus hudsonius
To 22 in. (55 cm)
Note white rump.

Black Vulture
Coragyps atratus
To 27 in. (68 cm)
Note white wing tips.

American Kestrel
Falco sparverius
To 12 in. (30 cm)
Note small size and blue wings.

Barred Owl
Strix varia
To 2 ft. (60 cm)
Call is a loud –
who-cooks-for-you?
who-cooks-for-you-all?

Bald Eagle
Haliaeetus leucocephalus
To 40 in. (1 m)

Great Horned Owl
Bubo virginianus
To 25 in. (63 cm)
Call is a resonant –
hoo-HOO-hoooo.

Eastern Screech-Owl
Megascops asio
To 9 in. (23 cm)
Small owl with ear tufts and yellow eyes.

Eastern Kingbird
Tyrannus tyrannus
To 8 in. (20 cm)
Note broad white tail band.

Great Crested Flycatcher
Myiarchus crinitus
To 9 in. (23 cm)

Acadian Flycatcher
Empidonax virescens
To 6 in. (15 cm)

Eastern Phoebe
Sayornis phoebe
To 7 in. (18 cm)
Wags its tail when perching.

Blue Jay
Cyanocitta cristata
To 14 in. (35 cm)

Eastern Wood-Pewee
Contopus virens
To 7 in. (18 cm)
Note 2 narrow white wing bars.

Red-winged Blackbird
Agelaius phoeniceus
To 9 in. (23 cm)

Horned Lark
Eremophila alpestris
To 8 in. (20 cm)

Brown-headed Cowbird
Molothrus ater
To 7 in. (18 cm)

Common Grackle
Quiscalus quiscula
To 14 in. (35 cm)

White-breasted Nuthatch
Sitta carolinensis
To 6 in. (15 cm)

Red-breasted Nuthatch
Sitta canadensis
To 4.5 in. (11 cm)

American Crow
Corvus brachyrhynchos
To 22 in. (55 cm)
Call is a distinct – caw.

European Starling
Sturnus vulgaris
To 9 in. (23 cm)

Common Raven
Corvus corax
To 27 in. (68 cm)
Call is a hoarse croak.

Cliff Swallow
Petrochelidon pyrrhonota
To 6 in. (15 cm)
Tail is square-edged.

Purple Martin
Progne subis
To 8 in. (20 cm)

Northern Rough-winged Swallow
Stelgidopteryx serripennis
To 6 in. (15 cm)
Note dusky throat.

Tree Swallow
Tachycineta bicolor
To 6 in. (15 cm)

Barn Swallow
Hirundo rustica
To 8 in. (20 cm)
Note deeply forked tail.

Eastern Meadowlark
Sturnella magna
To 9 in. (23 cm)

Black-capped Chickadee
Poecile atricapillus
To 6 in. (15 cm)
Name-saying call is –
chick-a-dee-dee-dee.

Red-eyed Vireo
Vireo olivaceus
To 6 in. (15 cm)

White-eyed Vireo
Vireo griseus
To 5 in. (13 cm)
Note white eye and yellow "spectacles."

House Wren
Troglodytes aedon
To 5 in. (13 cm)

Brown Creeper
Certhia americana
To 5 in. (13 cm)
Note downcurved bill.
Forages for insects on tree trunks.

Tufted Titmouse
Baeolophus bicolor
To 6 in. (15 cm)

Carolina Wren
Thryothorus ludovicianus
To 6 in. (15 cm)
Note white eyebrow stripe and wing bars.

Winter Wren
Troglodytes troglodytes
To 4 in. (10 cm)

Blue-gray Gnatcatcher
Polioptila caerulea
To 4.5 in. (11 cm)

Golden-crowned Kinglet
Regulus satrapa
To 3.5 in. (9 cm)

American Robin
Turdus migratorius
To 11 in. (28 cm)

Eastern Bluebird
Sialia sialis
To 7 in. (18 cm)

Hermit Thrush
Catharus guttatus
To 7 in. (18 cm)
Note rusty tail and spotted breast.

Wood Thrush
Hylocichla mustelina
To 8 in. (20 cm)

Cedar Waxwing
Bombycilla cedrorum
To 7 in. (18 cm)
Red wing marks look like waxy droplets.

Northern Mockingbird
Mimus polyglottos
To 11 in. (28 cm)

Brown Thrasher
Toxostoma rufum
To 12 in. (30 cm)

Gray Catbird
Dumetella carolinensis
To 9 in. (23 cm)
Repetitive call of variable sounds is interspersed with cat-like *mew* notes.

Baltimore Oriole
Icterus galbula
To 8 in. (20 cm)

Northern Parula
Setophaga americana
To 4.5 in. (11 cm)

Ovenbird
Seiurus aurocapilla
To 6 in. (15 cm)
Distinctive call is – tea-cher, tea-cher.

Black-throated Green Warbler
Setophaga virens
To 5 in. (13 cm)

Yellow-throated Warbler
Setophaga dominica
To 6 in. (15 cm)

Cerulean Warbler
Setophaga cerulea
To 4.5 in. (11 cm)
Note black neck ring.

Black-throated Blue Warbler
Setophaga caerulescens
To 6 in. (15 cm)

Hooded Warbler
Setophaga citrina
To 6 in. (15 cm)

Tennessee Warbler
Oreothlypis peregrina
To 5 in. (13 cm)
Plumage is greenish above and white below.

Chestnut-sided Warbler
Setophaga pensylvanica
To 5 in. (13 cm)
Note chestnut sides and yellow crown.

Prairie Warbler
Setophaga discolor
To 5 in. (13 cm)
Note black eye and cheek marks. Wags tail when perching.

Blue-winged Warbler
Vermivora cyanoptera
To 5 in. (13 cm)

Black-and-white Warbler
Mniotilta varia
To 6 in. (15 cm)
Note striped crown.

Yellow Warbler
Setophaga petechia
To 5 in. (13 cm)

Common Yellowthroat
Geothlypis trichas
To 5 in. (13 cm)

American Redstart
Setophaga ruticilla
To 5 in. (13 cm)

Kentucky Warbler
Geothlypis formosus
To 6 in. (15 cm)

Dark-eyed Junco
Junco hyemalis
To 7 in. (18 cm)
Four related "races" all have a dark hood and light outer tail feathers.

Yellow-breasted Chat
Icteria virens
To 7 in. (18 cm)
Note white "spectacles."

White-crowned Sparrow
Zonotrichia leucophrys
To 7 in. (18 cm)
White crown is bordered by black stripes.

Field Sparrow
Spizella pusilla
To 5 in. (13 cm)
Note pinkish bill.

House Sparrow
Passer domesticus
To 6 in. (15 cm)

White-throated Sparrow
Zonotrichia albicollis
To 7 in. (18 cm)
Note white throat and yellow spot in front of eye.

Song Sparrow
Melospiza melodia
To 7 in. (18 cm)
Note central breast spot.

American Goldfinch
Spinus tristis
To 5 in. (13 cm)

Pine Siskin
Spinus pinus
To 5 in. (13 cm)

Indigo Bunting
Passerina cyanea
To 6 in. (15 cm)

Northern Cardinal
Cardinalis cardinalis
To 9 in. (23 cm)
West Virginia's state bird.

Bobolink
Dolichonyx oryzivorus
To 8 in. (20 cm)

House Finch
Haemorhous mexicanus
To 6 in. (15 cm)

Scarlet Tanager
Piranga olivacea
To 7 in. (18 cm)

Eastern Towhee
Pipilo erythrophthalmus
To 9 in. (23 cm)

Rose-breasted Grosbeak
Pheucticus ludovicianus
To 9 in. (23 cm)

Summer Tanager
Piranga rubra
To 8 in. (20 cm)